The Wisdom of Jesus

His Life and Teachings in Calligraphy and Illustration

Collection by Thomas J. Moore

PAULIST PRESS
New York/Mahwah, N.J.

Acknowledgments: Scripture as indicated by "NIV" taken from the HOLY BIBLE: NEW INTER-
NATIONAL VERSION®. NIV® Copyright © 1973, 1978, 1984 by International Bible Society.
Used by permission of Zondervan Publishing House.
The NIV and "New International Version" trademarks are registered in the United States
Patent and Trademark Office by the International Bible Society.

New English Bible © Oxford University Press and
Cambridge University Press 1961, 1970. Used by permission.

The Scripture quotations contained within, as indicated by NRSV are from the New Revised
Standard Version Bible, copyright © 1989 by the Division of Christian Education of the
National Council of Churches of Christ in the U.S.A.,
and are used by permission. All rights reserved.

"The Golden Rule" by Norman Rockwell is printed by permission of the Norman Rockwell
Family Trust. Copyright © 1961 by the Norman Rockwell Family Trust.

Permission has been granted by the Discalced Carmelite Fathers, Munster,
Indiana, to reproduce photos taken by T. J. Moore in and around their shrine.

A special thanks is due Velma Woods, whose beautiful calligraphy helped inspire this book.

Cover design by Kokopelli Design Studio

Copyright © 1999 by Thomas J. Moore

Library of Congress Cataloging-in-Publication Data

Moore, Thomas J.,   1950–
The wisdom of Jesus : his life and teachings in calligraphy and illustration / collection by
Thomas J. Moore.
p.   cm.
Includes bibliographical references.
ISBN 0-8091-3909-X (alk. paper)
1. Jesus Christ Biography—Sources, Biblical. 2. Jesus Christ—Teachings. I. Title.
BT299.2.M66   1999
232.9′01—dc21
[B]   99-41159
CIP

BT
299.2
.M66
1999

Published by Paulist Press
997 Macarthur Boulevard
Mahwah, New Jersey 07430

www.paulistpress.com.

Printed and bound in the
United States of America

Contents

Abbreviations List

NIV   New International Version
NRSV   New Revised Standard Version
RSV   Revised Standard Version
KJV   King James Version
NEB   New English Bible

Photo Credits

Paulist Press gratefully acknowledges use of the photos used in this book.

p.   i: Jesus and Lamb courtsey of T. J. Moore
p.   2: Statue of Jesus courtesy of T. J. Moore
p.   4: Torah courtesy of T. J. Moore
p.   6: Lincoln…courtesy of T. J. Moore
p.   9: Stained Glass Nativity…courtesy of T. J. Moore
p. 10: Sunset…courtesy of T. J. Moore
p. 12: Madonna Mosaic…courtesy of Joseph Scott
p. 14: Stone Image of Star…courtesy of T. J. Moore
p. 16: Stone Angel…courtesy of T. J. Moore
p. 18: Candle…courtesy of Joseph Scott
p. 20: Head of Jesus…courtesy of T. J. Moore
p. 23: Jesus with Children…courtesy of T. J. Moore
p. 39: Jesus and Disciple…courtesy of T. J. Moore
p. 40: Jesus' Open Arms…courtesy of T. J. Moore
p. 42: Butterfly…courtesy of Animals, selected by Jim Harter, Dover Publications, N.Y. 1979.
p. 44: Boy with Big Eyes…courtesy of Discovery in Sight
p. 46: Deer…courtesy of T. J. Moore
p. 48: Ducks in pond…courtesy of T. J. Moore
p. 50: Stained Glass Dove…courtesy of T. J. Moore
p. 53: Shepherd's Face…courtesy of L. Boadt Collection
p. 54: Shepherd with Sheep…courtesy of L. Boadt Collection
p. 56: Jesus with Lamb…courtesy of T. J. Moore
p. 58: Baby and Blanket…courtesy of T. J. Moore
p. 60: Child in Carriage…courtesy of T. J. Moore
p. 62: Smiling Child…courtesy of T. J. Moore
p. 64: Family Scene…courtesy of Gail Denham
p. 66: Church…courtesy of T. J. Moore
p. 68: St. Francis Prayer…courtesy of T. J. Moore
p. 70: Norman Rockwell print…courtesy of Norman Rockwell Family Trust
p. 73: Stained Glass Agony in Garden…courtesy of T. J. Moore
p. 74: Church…courtesy of T. J. Moore
p. 76: Stone Relief of Last Supper…courtesy of T. J. Moore
p. 78: Stained Glass Feet…courtesy of T. J. Moore
p. 80: Tree…courtesy of Joseph Scott
p. 82: Jesus on Cross…courtesy of T. J. Moore
p. 84: Stained Glass, Woman at Jesus' Feet…courtesy of T. J. Moore
p. 86: Angel…courtesy of T. J. Moore
p. 88: Mountain, Flowers….courtesy of L. Boadt Collection
p. 90: Boy on Rock…courtesy of Joseph Scott
p. 92: Head of Jesus…courtesy of T. J. Moore
p. 95: Stalks of Grain…courtesy of Discovery in Sight
p. 96: Bird in the Air…courtesy of T. J. Moore
p. 98: Cross Quilt…courtesy of T. J. Moore
p. 100: Waterfall…courtesy of L. Boadt Collection
p. 102: Bible in Boat…courtesy of T. J. Moore
p. 104: Flowers…courtesy of T. J. Moore

Introduction

I have been a student and teacher of Bible study for a number of years. When teaching I have often used certain groupings of scripture to address a particular subject. I have recorded some of these in the form of calligraphy; it renders a certain grace and majesty appropriate to the verse.

I have attempted in this book to provide a brief overview of the life of Jesus Christ, and to present some of his major teachings. I have drawn most scripture from the Gospels (books Matthew, Mark, Luke and John of the New Testament); I have supplemented this with verses from the Old Testament, as well as verses from letters of the apostles John, Paul and Peter. Note that I have avoided making commentary about the scripture presented; I believe that faith is personal, and that each reader should form his or her own thoughts concerning each verse.

The first set of the teachings of Jesus (from "Friends" to "Everywhere We Are") provides basic concepts of Christian thought; these include faith, love, forgiveness, death and eternal life, inner peace. Some pieces reflect the nature of God in relation to the human person. The second set of teachings (from "Saving Grace" to "Love One Another") presents the message of salvation offered by Jesus to all peoples, and how this salvation may be obtained. It also reviews the character of Christian living, and how this affects our relationship with God, our family and all others.

I have constructed this book of scripture using several translations of the Bible (list on p. v). I have hopefully demonstrated that the power of the Word permeates all these translations, and it is best that the reader consult several sources when studying the Bible. I hope this book provides some new insights to those familiar with the teachings of Jesus, and serves as a good introduction to Christian thought for those of other faiths. "For everyone ought to know about Jesus Christ. No one ever lived, who was so good, so kind, so gentle" (Charles Dickens, 1849).

Full of Grace and Truth

The Word became flesh and lived for a while among us. We have seen his glory, the glory of the one and only Son, who came from the Father, full of grace and truth.

John 1:14 (NIV)

Thy Word

Thy word is a lamp unto my feet, and a light unto my path.

Psalm 119:105 (KJV)

One does not live by bread alone, but by every Word that comes from the mouth of the Lord.

Deuteronomy 8:3 (NRSV)

Do not think that I have come to abolish the Law or the Prophets; I have not come to abolish them but to fulfill them.

Jesus, Matthew 5:17 (NIV)

You shall love the Lord your God with all your heart, and with all your soul, and with all your mind. This is the great and first commandment. And the second is like it: You shall love your neighbor as yourself. On these two commandments depend all the Law and the Prophets.

Jesus, Matthew 22:37-40 (RSV)

Tree of Life

Happy are those...whose delight is in the law of the
    Lord....
They are like trees, planted by streams of water, which
    yield their fruit in its season, and their leaves do not
    wither.
In all that they do, they prosper.

                                Psalm 1:1-3 (NRSV)

The Birth of Christ

For God so loved the world, that he gave his only
    begotten Son, that whoever believeth in him should
    not perish, but have everlasting life.

John 3:16 (KJV)

Immanuel

Therefore the Lord himself shall give you a sign:
    Behold, a virgin shall conceive, and bear a son, and
    shall call his name Immanuel ("God with us").
                                        Isaiah 7:14 (KJV)

O Bethlehem

For this is what the prophet has written:
"And you, Bethlehem, in the land of Judah, are by no
  means least among the rulers of Judah; for out of
  you will come a ruler who is to shepherd my people
  Israel."

Matthew 2:5-6 (Micah 5:2) (NRSV)

And it came to pass in those days that a decree went
  out from Caesar Augustus that all the world should
  be registered...And all went to be registered,
  everyone to his own city. And Joseph also went up
  from Galilee, out of the city of Nazareth, into Judea,
  to the city of David, which is called Bethlehem,
  because he was of the house and lineage of David,
  to be registered with Mary, his espoused wife, who
  was with child. And so it was, that while they were
  there, the days were completed that she should be
  delivered. And she brought forth her firstborn son,
  and wrapped him in swaddling clothes and laid
  him in a manger, because there was no room for
  them in the inn.

Luke 2:1-7 (KJV)

Peace on Earth

An angel of the Lord stood before the shepherds, and the glory of the Lord shown around them, and they were terrified. But the angel said to them, "Do not be afraid; for see—I am bringing you good news of great joy for all the people: to you is born this day in the city of David a Savior, who is the Messiah, the Lord. This will be a sign for you: you will find a child wrapped in bands of cloth and lying in a manger."

And suddenly there was with the angel a multitude of the heavenly host, praising God and saying, "Glory to God in the highest heaven, and on earth peace among those whom God favors."

Luke 2:9-14 (NRSV)

Unto Us a Child is Born

The people walking in darkness have seen a great light;
    on those living in the land of the shadow of death,
    a light has dawned...
For unto us a child is born, to us a son is given,
    and the government will be on his shoulders.
And he will be called Wonderful Counselor,
    Mighty God,
Everlasting Father, Prince of Peace.
Of the increase of his government and peace, there will
    be no end.
He will reign on David's throne and over his kingdom,
    establishing
and upholding it with justice and righteousness
from that time on and forever.
The zeal of the Lord Almighty will accomplish this.

Isaiah 9:2, 6-7 (NIV)

Jesus went up to Nazareth. On the sabbath day he went
into the synagogue, as was his custom, and he
stood up to read, from the scroll of the prophet
Isaiah:
"The Spirit of the Lord is on me,
because he has anointed me to
preach good news to the poor.
He has sent me to proclaim freedom
for the prisoners and recovery
of sight for the blind,
to release the oppressed,
to proclaim the year of
the Lord's favor."
He rolled up the scroll, and said to those in the
synagogue, "Today this scripture is fulfilled in your
hearing."

Luke 4:16-21 (NIV)

The Teachings of Christ

FRIENDS

A friend loveth at all times.

Proverbs 17:17 (KJV)

This is my commandment, that you love one another
   as I have loved you. No one has greater love than
   this, to lay down one's life for one's friends. You are
   my friends if you do what I command you. I do not
   call you servants any longer, because the servant
   does not know what the master is doing; but I have
   called you friends, because I have made known to
   you everything that I have heard from my Father.
   You did not choose me but I chose you. And I
   appointed you to go and bear fruit, fruit that will
   last...."

Jesus, John 15:12-16 (NRSV)

THE LORD IS COMPASSIONATE

The Lord is compassionate and gracious,
    slow to anger, abounding in love.
He will not always accuse,
    nor will he harbor his anger forever;
he does not treat us as our sins deserve
or repay us according to our iniquities.
For as high as the heavens are above the earth,
    so great is his love for those who fear him;
as far as the east is from the west,
    so far has he removed our transgressions from us.
As a father has compassion on his children,
    so the Lord has compassion on those who fear him;
for he knows how we are formed,
    he remembers that we are dust.

                                Psalm 103:8-14 (NIV)

THE KINGDOM WITHIN

Behold, the kingdom of God lies within.

Luke 17:21 (KJV)

The kingdom of heaven (and faith) is like a mustard
seed, which a man took and planted in his field.
Though it is the smallest of all seeds, yet when it
grows, it is the largest of garden plants and
becomes a tree, so that the birds of the air come and
perch in its branches.

Matthew 13:31-32 (NIV)

As God's children, holy and dearly loved, clothe
yourselves with compassion, kindness, humility,
gentleness and patience. Bear with each other and
forgive whatever grievances you may have against
one another. Forgive as the Lord forgave you. And
over all these virtues put on love, which binds them
all together in perfect unity...Let the word of Christ
dwell within you richly.

Colossians 3:12-14, 16 (NIV)

LIGHT

The law of the Lord is perfect,
    reviving the soul.
The statutes of the Lord are
    trustworthy, making wise the simple.
The precepts of the Lord are right,
    giving joy to the heart.
The commands of the Lord are radiant,
    giving light to the eyes.

Psalm 19:7-8 (NIV)

If you do away with the yoke of oppression,
    with the pointing finger and malicious talk,
and if you spend yourselves in behalf
    of the hungry and satisfy the needs of the
    oppressed,
then your light will rise in the darkness,
    and your night will become like the noonday.
The Lord will guide you always.

Isaiah 58:9-11 (NIV)

Become the light of the world.

Jesus, Matthew 5:14 (NIV)

LOVE

The Lord is compassionate and gracious, slow to anger, abounding in love.

Psalm 103:8 (NIV)

For God so loved the world that He gave His one and only Son, that whoever believes in Him shall not perish but have life eternal.

John 3:16 (NIV)

I give you a new commandment: that you love one another. Just as I have loved you, you also should love one another. By this everyone will know that you are my disciples, if you have love for one another.

Jesus, John 13:34-35 (NRSV)

Love is patient, love is kind. It does not envy, it does not boast, it is not proud. It is not rude, it is not self-seeking, it is not easily angered, it keeps no record of wrongs. Love does not delight in evil but rejoices with the truth. It always protects, always trusts, always hopes, always perseveres. Love never fails.

1 Corinthians 13:4-8 (NIV)

For I am convinced that neither death nor life, neither angels nor demons, neither the present nor the future, nor any powers, neither height nor depth, nor anything else in all creation, will be able to separate us from the love of God that is in Christ Jesus our Lord.

Romans 8:38-39 (NIV)

MERCY

What does the Lord require of you?
To act justly and to love mercy,
and to walk humbly with your God.

Micah 6:8 (NIV)

Go and learn what this means:
"I desire mercy, not sacrifice."

Jesus, Matthew 9:13 (NIV)

passages on mercy:
    the proper fast (Isaiah 58:6-10)
    the good samaritan (Luke 10:25-37)
    serving God by serving others (Matthew 25:34-40)

Be perfect, therefore, as your heavenly Father is perfect.
Be merciful, just as your heavenly Father is merciful.

Jesus, Matthew 5:38 & Luke 6:36 (NIV)

Let us not love with words or tongue,
but with action and in truth.

1 John 3:18 (NIV)

PRAYER

May the words of my mouth and the
    meditations of my heart
        be pleasing in your sight.
O Lord, my Rock and my Redeemer.

Psalm 19:14 (NIV)

I pray that you may have the power, together with all
    the saints, to grasp how wide and long and high
    and deep is the love of Christ, and to know this love
    that surpasses knowledge—that you may be filled to
    the measure of all the fullness of God.

Paul, Ephesians 3:17-19 (NIV)

Above all, maintain constant love for one another, for
    love covers a multitude of sins. Be hospitable to one
    another without complaining. Like good stewards of
    the manifold grace of God, serve one another with
    whatever gift each of you has received. Whoever
    speaks must do so as one speaking the very words
    of God; whoever serves must do so with the
    strength that God supplies, so that God may be
    glorified in all things through Jesus Christ.

1 Peter 4:8-11 (NRSV)

O righteous Father, though the world does not know
    you, I know you; and these disciples know that you
    have sent me. I have made you known to them,
    and will continue to make you known in order that
    the love you have for me may be in them, and that
    I myself may be in them.

Jesus, John 17:25-26 (NIV)

FORGIVENESS

I did not come to judge the world, but to save it!
                                          John 12:47 (NIV)

Judge not, and you will not be judged. Condemn not,
   and you will not be condemned. Forgive and you
   will be forgiven.
                                          Luke 6:37 (RSV)

Let anyone among you who is without sin be the first
   to throw a stone.
                                          John 8:7 (NRSV)

Forgive anyone who offends you not seven times, but
   seventy times seven.
                                          Matthew 18:22 (NRSV)

Father, forgive them, for they know not what they do.
                                    Christ crucified, Luke 23:34 (RSV)

Carry this message of repentance and forgiveness of
   sins to all nations.... And surely I will be with you
   always, to the very end of the age.
                                    Christ risen, Matthew 28:19-20 (NIV)

PEACE

The Lord is near. Do not be anxious about anything, but in everything, by prayer and petition, with thanksgiving, present your requests to God. And the peace of God which transcends all understanding will guard your hearts and minds in Christ Jesus.
                                        Philippians 4:5-7 (NIV)

this peace comes from:
  – assurance of the continued love of Jesus
    (Matthew 28:20; Romans 8:35-39)
  – freedom from death (Revelation 21:3-4)
  – the promise of heaven (John 14:2)
  – freedom from worry (Matthew 6:25-33)
  – rest for the weary (Matthew 11:28-30)
  – and strength (Isaiah 40:31)

we are to share this peace:
Praise be to the God and Father of our Lord Jesus Christ, the Father of compassion and the God of all comfort, who comforts us in all our troubles, so that we can comfort those in any trouble with the comfort we ourselves have received from God. For just as the sufferings of Christ flow over into our lives, so also through Christ our comfort overflows.
                                        2 Corinthians 1:3-5 (NIV)

LIFE ETERNAL

For God so loved the world, that he gave his only-
begotten Son, that whoever believeth in him should
not perish, but have everlasting life.

John 3:16 (KJV)

Do not let your hearts be troubled. In my Father's house
are many rooms; if it were not so, I would have told
you. I am going there to prepare a place for you.
And if I go and prepare a place for you, I will come
back and take you to be with me that you may also
be where I am. You know the way to the place
where I am going.

Jesus, John 14:1-4 (NIV)

Behold, God's dwelling is with the human race. He will
dwell with them and they will be his people and
God himself will always be with them (as their
God). He will wipe away every tear from their eyes,
and there shall be no more death or mourning,
wailing or pain, (for) the old has passed away.

Revelation 21:3-4 (NRSV)

EVERYWHERE WE ARE

Dear Lord, where can I go from your Spirit? Where can
   I flee from your presence? If I go up to the heavens,
   you are there; if I make my bed in the depths, you
   are there. If I rise on the wings of dawn, if I settle on
   the far side of the sea, even there your hand will
   guide me, your right hand will hold me fast.
                                        Psalm 139:7-10 (NIV)

The Lord watches over you—
      he is the shade at your right hand;
the sun will not harm you by day,
      nor the moon by night.
The Lord will keep you from all harm—
      he will watch over your life;
the Lord will watch over your coming
      and going both now and forevermore.
                                        Psalm 121:5-8 (NIV)

Surely I will be with you always, to the very end of the
   age.
                                   Jesus, Matthew 28:20 (NIV)

THE LORD'S PRAYER

My house shall be called a house of prayer, a house of
prayer for all peoples, thus says the Lord.

Isaiah 56:7 (NRSV)

Jesus was praying in a certain place, and after he had
finished, one of his disciples said to him "Lord, teach
us to pray."
He said to them, "When you pray, say:
Our Father who art in heaven, hallowed by thy name.
Thy kingdom come. Thy will be done, on earth as it
is in heaven. Give us this day our daily bread. And
forgive us our trespasses, as we forgive those who
trespass against us. And lead us not into temptation,
but deliver us from evil." (For thine is the kingdom
and the power and the glory forever. Amen)

The Lord's Prayer, Luke 11:1-4 (KJV)

BLESSINGS

The Lord is gracious and merciful, slow to anger and
    abounding in steadfast love.
The Lord is good to all, and his compassion is over all
    that he has made.

                                    Psalm 145:8-9 (NIV)

Blessed are the poor in spirit, for theirs is the kingdom
    of heaven.
Blessed are those who mourn, for they shall be
    comforted.
Blessed are the meek, for they will inherit the earth.
Blessed are those who hunger and thirst for
    righteousness,
    for they shall be filled.
Blessed are the merciful, for they shall receive mercy.
Blessed are the pure in heart, for they will see God.
Blessed are the peacemakers, for they shall be called
    children of God.
Blessed are those who are persecuted for righteousness'
    sake, for theirs is the kingdom of heaven.

                                  Matthew 5:1-10 (NRSV)

Jesus' Message of Salvation

Saving Grace

This is indeed the will of my Father, that all who see the Son and believe in him may have eternal life; and I will raise them up on the last day.

Jesus, John 6:40 (NRSV)

God, rich in mercy, for the great love he bore us, brought us to life with Christ even when we were dead in our sins; it is by his grace you are saved.

Ephesians 2:4-5 (NEB)

The word is near you: it is in your mouth and in your heart... If you confess with your mouth, "Jesus is Lord," and believe in your heart that God raised him from the dead, you will be saved. For it is with your heart that you believe and are justified, and it is with your mouth that you confess and are saved.

Romans 10:8-10 (NIV)

Born Again

Jesus declared: "Very truly, I tell you, no one can see the
  kingdom of God without being born from above...
  no one can enter the kingdom of God without being
  born of water and Spirit. What is born of the flesh
  is flesh, and what is born of the Spirit is spirit."

John 3:3-6 (NRSV)

If any want to become my followers, let them deny
  themselves and take up their cross and follow me.
  For those who want to save their life will lose it,
  and those who lose their life for my sake, and
  for the sake of the gospel, will save it. For what
  will it profit them to gain the whole world and
  forfeit their life?

Jesus, Mark 8:34-36 (NRSV)

So if anyone is in Christ, there is a new creation:
  everything old has passed away; see, everything
  has become new!

2 Corinthians 5:17 (NRSV)

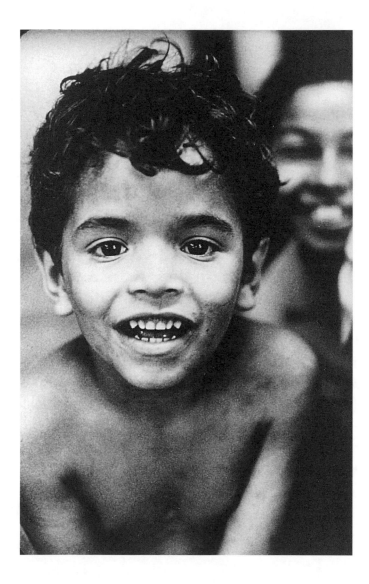

Eyes of the Heart

The commands of the Lord are radiant, giving light to
the eyes.

Psalm 19:8 (NIV)

Blessed are your eyes because they see, and your ears
because they hear.

Jesus, Matthew 13:16 (NIV)

The eye is the lamp of the body. If your eyes are good,
your whole body will be filled with light. But if your
eyes are bad, your whole body will be filled with
darkness.

Jesus, Matthew 6:22-23 (NIV)

I pray that the eyes of your heart may be enlightened in
order that you may know the hope to which Christ
has called you...that you may have the power to
grasp how wide and long and high and deep is the
love of Christ, and to know this love that surpasses
knowledge.

Ephesians 1:18 and 3:18-19 (NIV)

Freedom

The Lord is the Spirit, and where the Spirit of the Lord
   is there is freedom.

2 Corinthians 3:17 (NIV)

Then Jesus said to the Jews who believed in him, "If
   you continue in my word, you are truly my
   disciples; and you will know the truth, and the truth
   will make you free."
They answered him, "We are the descendants of
   Abraham and have never been slaves to anyone.
   What do you mean by saying 'you will be made
   free'?"
Jesus answered them: "Very truly, I tell you, everyone
   who commits sin is a slave to sin. The slave does
   not have a permanent place in the household; the
   son has a place there forever. So if the Son makes
   you free, you will be free indeed."

John 8:31-36 (NRSV)

Our Father Provides

Therefore I tell you, do not worry about your life, what
 you will eat or drink, or about your body, what you
 will wear. Is not life more important than food, and
 the body more important than clothes? Look at the
 birds of the air; they do not sow or reap or store
 away in barns, and yet your heavenly Father feeds
 them. Are you not much more valuable than they?
 Who of you by worrying can add a single hour to
 his life?...
Seek first the kingdom of my Father and his
 righteousness, and all these (material) things will be
 given to you as well.

Jesus, Matthew 6:25-27 & 33 (NIV)

Treasures in Heaven

No one can serve two masters; for a slave will either hate the one and love the other, or be devoted to the one and despise the other. You cannot serve God and wealth.

Jesus, Matthew 6:24 (NRSV)

Do not store up for yourselves treasures on earth, where moth and rust destroy, and where thieves break in and steal. But store up for yourselves treasures in heaven, where moth and rust do not destroy, and where thieves do not break in and steal. For where your treasure is, there your heart will also be.

Matthew 6:19-21 (NIV)

The Good Shepherd

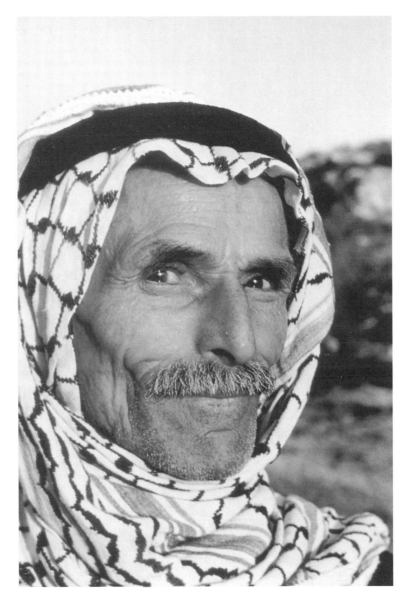

The Good Shepherd

The Lord is my shepherd, I shall not want;
he makes me lie down in green pastures.
He leads me beside still waters;
    he restores my soul.
He leads me in paths of righteousness
      for his name's sake.

Psalm 23 (RSV)

The one who enters by the gate is the shepherd...he calls
     his own sheep by name and leads them out...and
     the sheep follow him because they know his voice....
I am the good shepherd....
Very truly, I tell you, I am the gate for the sheep.
     ...whoever enters by me will be saved, and will
     come in and go out and find pasture.

John 10:2, 4, 7-8, 11 (NRSV)

Of Lost Sheep

Seek the Lord while he may be found,
call upon him while he is near;
let the wicked forsake their way
and the unrighteous their thoughts;
let them return to the Lord,
that he may have mercy on them,
and to our God, for he will abundantly pardon.

Isaiah 55:6-7 (NRSV)

Jesus told them this parable: "Which one of you,
having a hundred sheep and losing one of them,
does not leave the ninety-nine in the wilderness and
go after the one that is lost until he finds it? When
he has found it, he lays it on his shoulders and
rejoices. And when he comes home, he calls together
his friends and neighbors, saying to them, 'Rejoice
with me, for I have found my sheep that was lost.'
Just so, I tell you, there will be more joy in heaven
over one sinner who repents than over ninety-nine
righteous persons who need no repentance."

Luke 15:3-7 (NRSV)

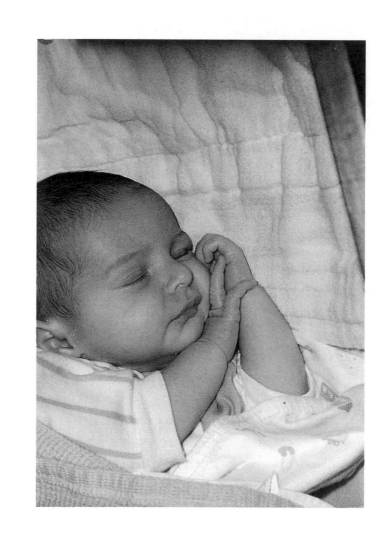

Children

Jesus told his disciples, "Let the little children come to me, and do not hinder them, for the kingdom of God belongs to such as these. I tell you the truth, anyone who will not receive the kingdom of God like a little child will never enter it." And he took the children in his arms, put his hands on them and blessed them.

Mark 10:13-16 (NIV)

Children of God

The disciples came to Jesus and asked, "Who is the
 greatest in the kingdom of heaven?" He called a
 child, whom he put among them, and said, "Truly I
 tell you, unless you change and become like children
 you will never enter the kingdom of heaven.
 Whoever becomes humble like this child is the
 greatest in the kingdom of heaven. Whoever
 welcomes one such child in my name welcomes
 me.
"If any of you put a stumbling block before one of these
 little ones who believes in me, it would be better for
 you if a great millstone were fastened around your
 neck, and you were drowned in the depth of the sea.
 Woe to the world because of stumbling blocks!
 Occasions for stumbling are bound to come, but
 woe to the one by whom the stumbling block
 comes!
"Take care that you do not despise one of these little
 ones; for I tell you, in heaven their angels
 continually see the face of my Father in heaven."
                              Matthew 18:1-7, 10 (NRSV)

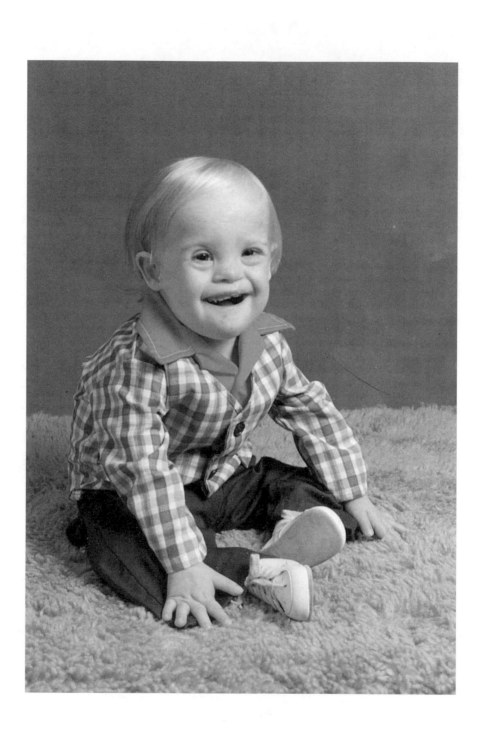

God's Special Children

God has made everything beautiful in its time.
He has set eternity in the hearts of all.
Ecclesiastes 3:11 (NRSV)

Family

A father to the fatherless, a defender of widows, is God
in his holy dwelling. He sets the lonely in families...
Psalm 68:5-6 (NIV)

God has said: "I will live with them and walk among
them, and I will be their God, and they will be my
people... I will be a Father to them, and they will be
my sons and daughters."
2 Corinthians 6:16-18 (NIV)

In Christ Jesus you are all children of God through faith.
Galatians 3:26 (NRSV)

They who have my commandments and keep them are
those who love me; and those who love me will be
loved by my Father, and I will love them and reveal
myself to them.
Jesus, John 14:21 (NRSV)

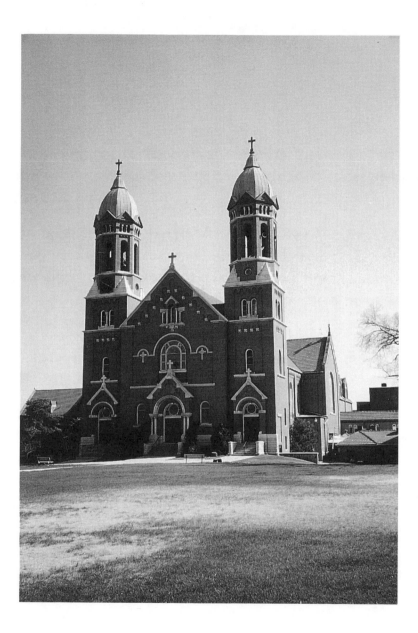

The Vine

I am the real vine, and my Father is the gardener.
Every barren branch of mine he cuts away; and
every fruiting branch he cleans, to make it more
fruitful still. You have already been cleansed by the
word that I spoke to you. Dwell in me, as I in you.
No branch can bear fruit by itself, but only if it
remains with the vine; no more can you bear fruit
unless you remain united with me...
If you dwell in me and my words dwell in you, ask
what you will, and you shall have it. This is to my
Father's glory, that you may bear fruit in plenty
and so be my disciples.

Jesus, John 15:1-18 (NEB)

Make every effort to keep the unity of the Spirit through
the bond of peace. There is one body and one Spirit—
just as you are called to one hope when you were
called—one Lord, one faith, one baptism, one God
and Father of all, who is over all and through all
and in all.

Ephesians 4:3-6 (NIV)

Bread of Life

Jesus said to them, "I am the bread of life. Whoever
    comes to me will never be hungry, and whoever
    believes in me will never be thirsty... Everything
    that the Father gives me will come to me, and
    anyone who comes to me I will never drive away."
                           John 6:35,37 (NRSV)

I did not come to judge the world, but to save it!
                           John 12:47 (NIV)

Do not judge:
    the sinner (1 John 1:8,9; John 8:2-11)
    one's enemy (Matthew 5:38-48)
    an alien or stranger (Galatians 3:26-28; Hebrews 13:1-2)
    one of differing faith or beliefs (Romans 14:1-18)
    the downtrodden (Isaiah 58:10-11; Matthew 25:31-40)

Whoever does the will of my Father in heaven is my
    brother and sister and mother.
                     Jesus, Matthew 12:50 (NIV)

My command is this: love one another.
Jesus, John 13:34 (NIV)

The Death and Resurrection of Christ

A Single Grain

I tell you truly, unless a grain of wheat falls into the
earth and dies, it remains just a single grain; but if
it dies, it bears much fruit.

Jesus, John 12:24 (NRSV)

The Last Supper

When the hour came, Jesus and his apostles reclined at
the table. And he said to them, "I have eagerly
desired to eat this Passover with you before I suffer.
For I tell you, I will not eat it again until it finds
fulfillment in the kingdom of God…"
He took bread, gave thanks and broke it, and gave it to
them, saying, "This is my body given for you; do
this in remembrance of me."
In the same way, he took the cup saying, "This cup is
the new covenant in my blood, which is poured out
for you."

Luke 22:14-20 (NIV)

Jesus told his disciples, "In a little while you will see me
no more, and then after a little while you will see
me. What do I mean by this? I tell you the truth,
you will weep and mourn while the world rejoices.
You will grieve, but your grief will turn to joy. A
woman giving birth to a child has pain because her
time has come; but when her baby is born she
forgets the anguish because of her joy that a child is
brought into the world. So with you: Now is your
time of grief, but I will see you again and you will
rejoice, and no one will take away your joy."

John 16:16-22 (NIV)

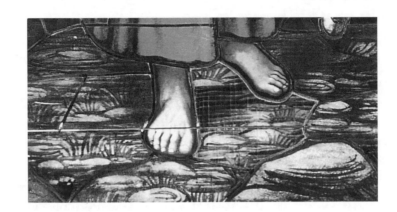

Master and Servant

During supper Jesus...got up from the table...poured
water into a basin and began to wash the disciples'
feet...he said, "You do not know now what I am
doing, but later you will understand...unless I wash
you, you have no share with me."

After Jesus had washed their feet...and had returned to
the table, he said to them, "Do you know what I
have done to you? You call me Teacher and Lord—
and you are right, for that is what I am. So if I,
your Lord and Teacher, have washed your feet, you
also ought to wash one another's feet. For I have set
you an example, that you also should do as I have
done to you. Very truly, I tell you, servants are not
greater than their master, nor are messengers
greater than the one who sent them. If you know
these things, you are blessed if you do them.

John 13:5-8, 12-17 (NRSV)

In the Garden

O righteous Father, though the world does not know
you, I know you; and these disciples know that you
have sent me. I have made you known to them,
and will continue to make you known in order that
the love you have for me may be in them, and that
I myself may be in them.

Jesus, John 17:25-26 (NIV)

When they came to the place that is called Golgotha,
   the soldiers crucified Jesus with the criminals, one
   on his right and one on his left. And they cast lots to
   divide his clothing. And the people stood by,
   watching; but the leaders scoffed at him, saying,
   "He saved others; let him save himself if he is the
   Messiah of God, his chosen one!"
One of the criminals who hung there derided Jesus and
   said, "Are you not the Christ? Save yourself and
   us!" but the other rebuked him, saying, "Do you not
   fear God, since you are under the same sentence of
   death? We indeed have been condemned justly, for
   we are getting what we deserve for our deeds, but
   this man has done nothing wrong." Then he said,
   "Jesus, remember me when you come into your
   kingdom." Jesus replied, "Truly, today you will be
   with me in Paradise."
It was now about the sixth hour (noon), and darkness
   came over the whole land until the ninth hour, for
   the sun's light failed. And the curtain of the temple
   was torn in two. Then Jesus, calling out with a loud
   voice, said, "Father, into your hands I commend my
   spirit." Having said this, he breathed his last.

Luke 25:33-46 (NRSV)

Surely he has borne our infirmities
and carried our diseases;
yet we accounted him stricken,
struck down by God, and afflicted.
But he was wounded for our transgressions,
crushed for our iniquities;
upon him was the punishment that made us whole,
and by his bruises we are healed.
All we like sheep have gone astray;
we have all turned to our own way
and the Lord has laid on him
the iniquity of us all.

Isaiah 53:4-6 (NRSV)

The Empty Tomb

After the sabbath, as the first day of the week was dawning, Mary Magdalene and the other Mary went to see the tomb. And suddenly there was a great earthquake; for an angel of the Lord, descending from heaven, came and rolled back the stone and sat upon it. His appearance was like lightning, and his clothing white as snow. The angel said to the women: "Do not be afraid, for I know that you are looking for Jesus, who was crucified. He is not here; he has risen, just as he said. Come and see the place where he lay. Then go quickly and tell his disciples: 'He has risen from the dead and is going ahead of you into Galilee. There you will see him.' This is my message."

Matthew 28:1-7 (NRSV)

I am the resurrection and the life. Those who believe in me, even though they die, will live, and everyone who lives and believes in me will never die.

John 11:25-26 (NRSV)

The Easter Message

I have come that you may have life, and have it
    abundantly...

John 10:10 (NRSV)

This is the will of my Father, that all who see the Son
    and believe in him shall have eternal life; and I will
    raise them up on the last day.

Jesus, John 6:40 (NRSV)

All authority in heaven and on earth has been given to me. Therefore, go and make disciples of all nations, baptizing them in the name of the Father and of the Son and of the Holy Spirit, and teaching them to obey everything I have commanded you. And surely I will be with you always, to the very end of the age.

Jesus, the Great Commission,
Matthew 28:18-20 (NIV)

Conclusion

Sending the Holy Spirit

I will ask the Father, and he will give you another
    Counselor, to be with you forever. This is the Spirit
    of truth, whom the world cannot receive, because it
    neither sees him nor knows him. You know him,
    because he abides with you, and he will be in you.
I will not leave you as orphans; I am coming to you. In
    a little while the world will no longer see me, but
    you will see me; because I live, you also will live.
                                Jesus, John 14:16-19 (NIV)

We know that we live in him (Jesus) and he in us,
    because he has given us of his Spirit. And we have
    seen and testify that the Father has sent his Son to
    be the Savior of the world.
                                    1 John 4:13-14 (NIV)

Taking Up the Cross

If any want to become my followers, let them deny
themselves and take up their cross and follow me.
For those who want to save their life will lose it, and
those who lose their life for my sake will find it.
What will it profit them if they gain the whole
world but forfeit their life?

Jesus, Matthew 16:24-26 (NRSV)

In this world you will have trials and tribulation. But
take heart! I have overcome the world.

Jesus, John 16:33 (NIV)

If you suffer for doing good and you endure it, this is
commendable before God. To this you were called,
because Christ suffered for you, leaving you an
example, that you should follow in his steps.

1 Peter 2:20, 21 (NIV)

The God of all grace, who called you to his eternal glory
in Christ, after you have suffered a little while, will
himself restore you and make you strong, firm and
steadfast.

1 Peter 5:10 (NIV)

As One Approved

Happy are those who do not follow the advice of the wicked, or take the path that sinners tread, or sit in the seat of the scoffers; but their delight is in the law of the Lord, and on his law they meditate day and night. They are like trees planted by streams of water, which yield their fruit in its season, and their leaves do not wither. In all that they do, they prosper.

Psalm 1:1-3 (NRSV)

Do your best to present yourself to God as one approved by him, a worker who has no need to be ashamed, rightly explaining the word of truth. Avoid profane chatter...all who cleanse themselves of the things I have mentioned will become special utensils, dedicated and useful to the owner of the house, ready for every good work.

2 Timothy 2:15-16, 21 (NRSV)

Ambassadors for Christ

So, if anyone is in Christ, there is a new creation:
everything old has passed away; see, everything
has become new! All this is from God, who
reconciled himself to us through Christ, and has
given us the ministry of reconciliation; that is, in
Christ God was reconciling the world to himself, not
counting their trespasses against them, and
entrusting the message of reconciliation to us. So we
are ambassadors for Christ...

2 Corinthians 5:17-20 (NRSV)

Miracles

Jesus passed along the sea of Galilee and went up the
mountain, where he sat down. Great crowds came
to him, bringing with them the lame, the maimed,
the blind, the mute, and many others. They put
them at his feet, and he cured them, so that the
crowd was amazed when they saw the mute
speaking, the maimed whole, the lame walking,
and the blind seeing. And they praised the God of
Israel.

Matthew 15:29-31 (NRSV)

Very truly, I tell you, the one who believes in me will
also do the works that I do and, in fact, will do
greater works than these, because I am going to the
Father. I will do whatever you ask in my name, so
that the Father may be glorified in the Son. If in my
name you ask me for anything, I will do it.

Jesus, John 14:12-14 (NRSV)